Ella Loves ELVIS

Dedicated to Joan Jones

"Thank you, Fontaine Wallace, my wonderful mother and editor." - M.W.C.

Find my books at Amazon, Barnes & Noble, Walmart, IngramSpark, and more!

www.MicheleWallaceCampanelli.com

www.ThePictureBookPro.org

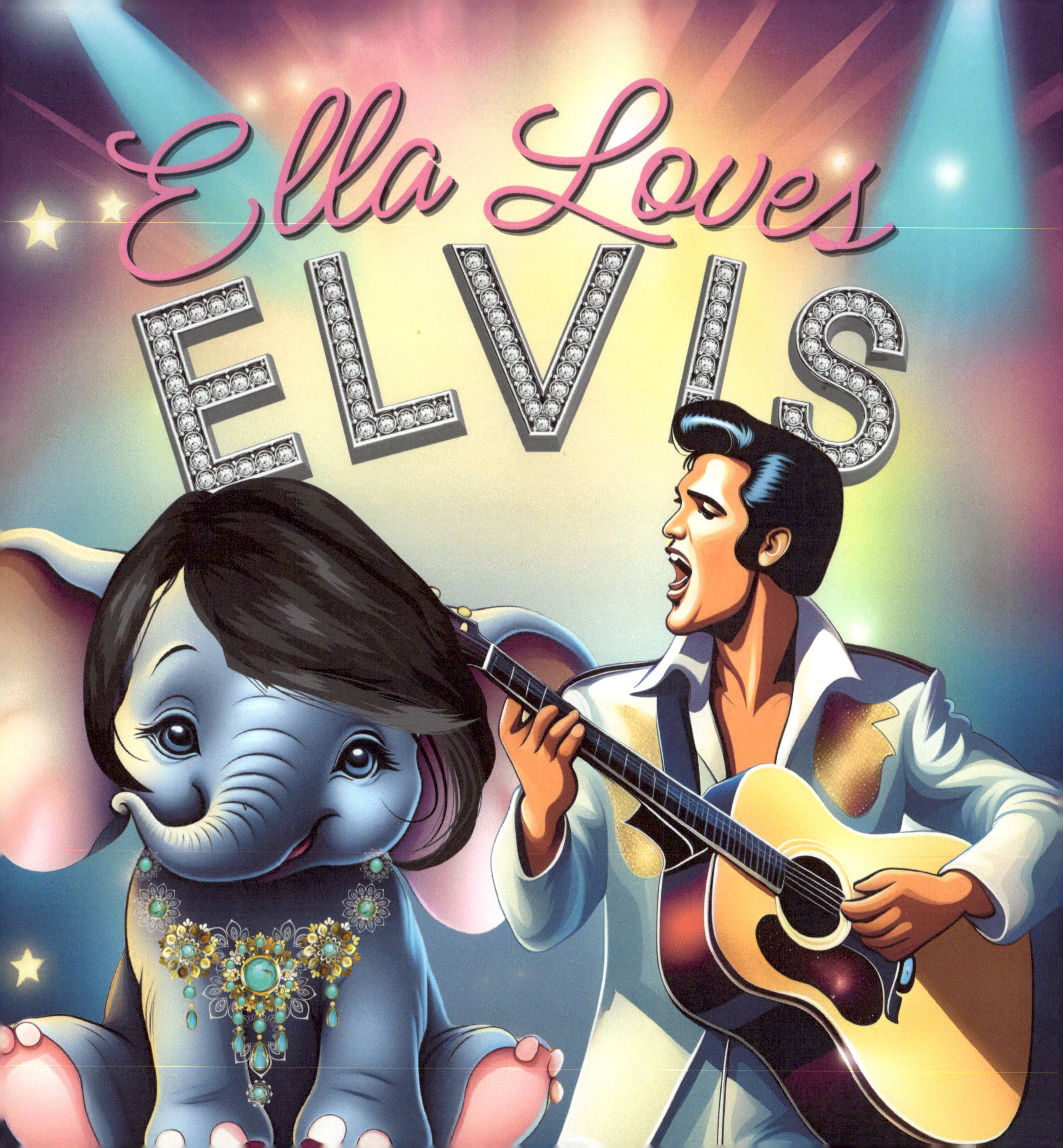

Ella Loves
ELVIS

Katy loved animals. Her farm, "Rushing River Rescue Farm," was next to the Indian River and its 12 acres was home to many different types of rescues such as horses, cows, goats, donkeys and one pig named Baxter.

Everyone in the community loved and respected this farm and knew it was struggling. Katy never regretted saving animals even though the expense for feeding was enormous. She enjoyed taking care of them like family.

There was only one time she questioned her decision to rescue an animal and that is when the local circus called and asked if she could take in a baby elephant.

Yes, a baby named Ella. The circus was closing due to protests and Ella was underweight because Ella's mother was being mistreated and rejected her. The circus was feeding it by bottles, but they just didn't have the skill or workers available to take on this huge task. The circus manager stressed that Ella was a handful.

At first, things seemed to go well. Ella drank from the bottle and had a huge pasture to play in. However, the other animals stayed away from Ella. Usually social, even the mini cows would not go near Ella. In fact, after a few days, Ella hadn't made any friends on the farm. The little baby elephant began to show signs of sadness especially after she approached Baxter, and the pig ran off squealing back into the barn.

Katy wondered if the animals didn't like that Ella because they had never seen a circus elephant before. Perhaps her size brought fear. Katy thought that was it until she moved Ella into the barn and heard the cries of fear from the horses and goats. After an hour, she had no choice but to move Ella back to the pasture. The barn animals calmed down; it was then that Katy saw tears in Ella's eyes, perhaps tears of rejection.

Katy called the circus owner in hopes of finding a way for Ella to become happier living on the farm or to return her. The circus owner was surprised to hear from Katy. "I am sorry you think Ella is unhappy there," the Circus owner said.

"The cost of keeping Ella was starting to eat me out of house and home. She eats so much."

"Finding a solution to Ella's happiness is easy. Ella loves Elvis' music. I used to play Elvis during her training," the Circus owner said. "She will brighten right up."

"Ok, thanks for the tip. I can get an Elvis CD from my mom. However, that still doesn't solve the financial strain."

"I tried to warn you. Why don't you sell one of your ponies?"

"They aren't ponies," Katy stressed. "We have mini horses, and we need them for the upcoming spring festival."

CIRCUS

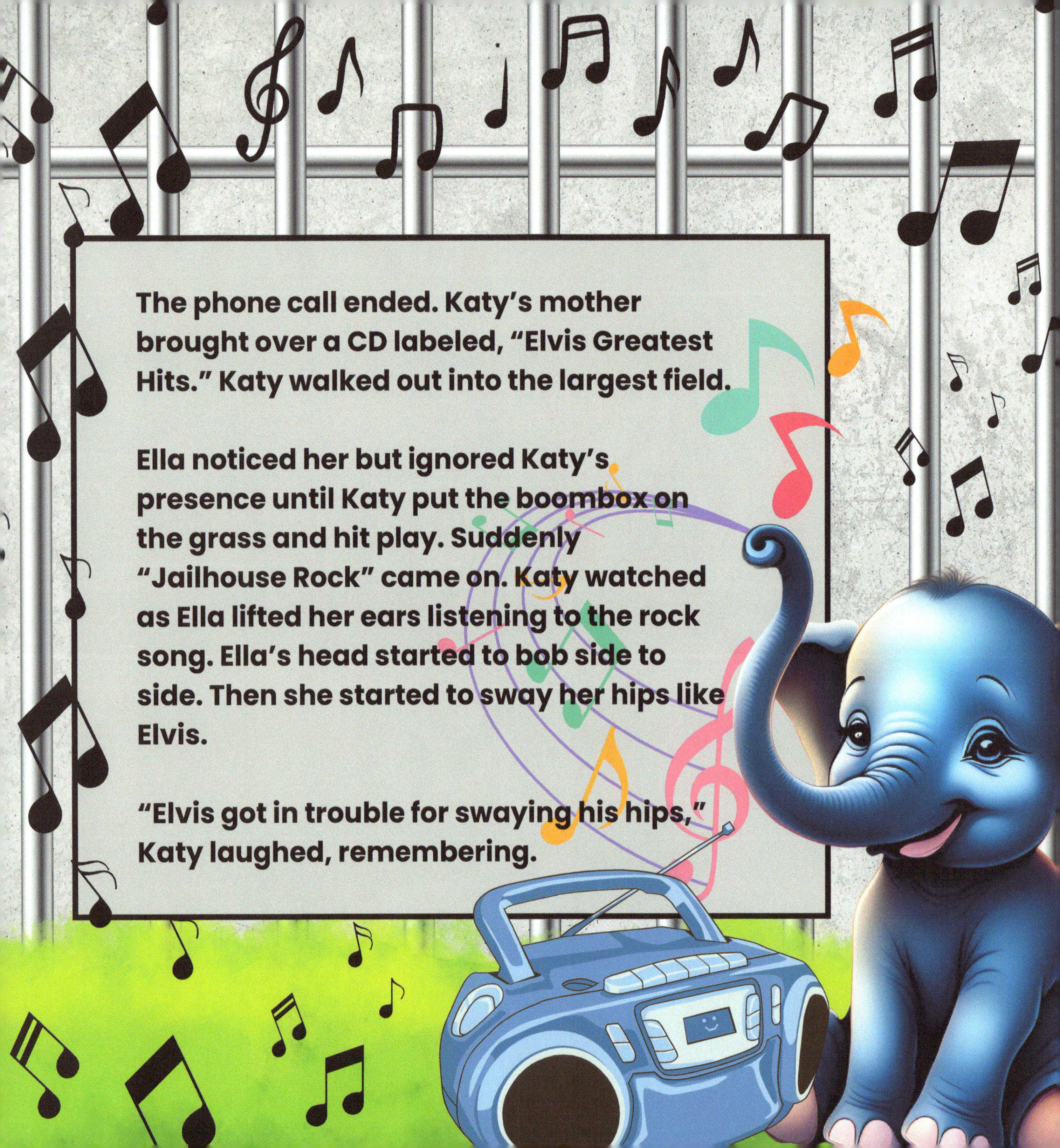

The phone call ended. Katy's mother brought over a CD labeled, "Elvis Greatest Hits." Katy walked out into the largest field.

Ella noticed her but ignored Katy's presence until Katy put the boombox on the grass and hit play. Suddenly "Jailhouse Rock" came on. Katy watched as Ella lifted her ears listening to the rock song. Ella's head started to bob side to side. Then she started to sway her hips like Elvis.

"Elvis got in trouble for swaying his hips," Katy laughed, remembering.

Elvis Presley
Jailhouse Rock
Elvis Presley

Ella swayed faster which caused Katy to laugh. Then the song changed to "Can't Help Falling in Love With You," and the goats and mini-Highland cows started heading toward the pasture out of the barn.

Katy thought they were headed toward the hay, but instead, they kept on going to the fence to watch Ella and listen to Elvis. All their ears were perked up and they seemed to be interested. Ella bent down on one knee as if pledging her love through Elvis' voice. The animals were shaking their hips, bouncing and nodding to the beat of the music. They were making so much noise Katy's husband came out of the barn.

Suddenly, he dropped to his knees laughing and watching the animals. "I didn't realize we were having a party," he laughed.

"They all seem to like the music," Katy said.

Ella trotted over to her pile of food and grabbed an apple with her trunk. She tossed it to Baxter the pig who immediately ate it. "Ella's finally making friends," Katy said, happily.

Baxter headed towards Ella for more treats and Ella gladly gave away another apple. A few minutes later, Ella also gave the goats treats. The animals were sharing food and dancing to Elvis.

Katy's husband suddenly went to his feet and took Katy in his arms and started dancing. Katy was shocked because they hadn't danced since their wedding over a decade ago. She took a deep breath and enjoyed the moment. She loved being in his arms. His eyes were green like emeralds, and they were looking back at her with such joy.

"This is fun!" her husband announced.

"It is," Katy smiled.

"I think we found a way to keep Ella," he said.

"But she is very expensive even if she is making friends," Katy added happily. Music can help do so.

"With the fair coming up, we can enter Ella in the talent contest and win the money. She can earn the money to keep the farm going," the husband said, hugging his wife.

He leaned down and kissed her. It seemed like a magical kiss that made Katy's heart swell and melt all her troubles away.

"Do you really think we can win?" Katy asked.

The husband grinned. "You can put your sewing to work too by making a bedazzled elephant coat."

Katy suddenly exclaimed, "I could even make a wig out of that old black shag carpet in the shed!"

They laughed as all the animals danced to, "All Shook Up."

The farmer's wife felt, since Ella loved Elvis, maybe she should teach her a little about him. She ordered a book from Graceland which is the USA's most visited private home. She not only got the book, but when it arrived, she carried it out onto the field and sat down to read it. Ella came over and looked over her shoulder at the big pictures of Elvis in concert. Ella looked at every page turn and bobbed her head. When the farmer's wife read an Elvis fact, Ella would trumpet like saying "Way to go", such as when she said, "Elvis has over 150 albums, holds the most top 40 hits, sold over 1 billion records, starred in 31 movies, actually, it was 32 because he was seen in Die Hard according to Bruce Willis," added the wife.

"Elvis won 3 Gospel Grammys, had two US Postal stamps honoring him and served 6 years in the army with 2 being active duty." Then the wife read, "He had one daughter, Lisa Marie," and Ella trumpeted her agreement. The next page mentioned his death, but the farmer's wife closed the book, "I will read about that later. With so many fans, Elvis will never die. He'll always be the King of Rock-N-Roll. He continues to remain a popular artist due to rock fusion with other genres of music, his close connection with audiences, his ability to overcome social divides as a global icon who transcends all popular culture."

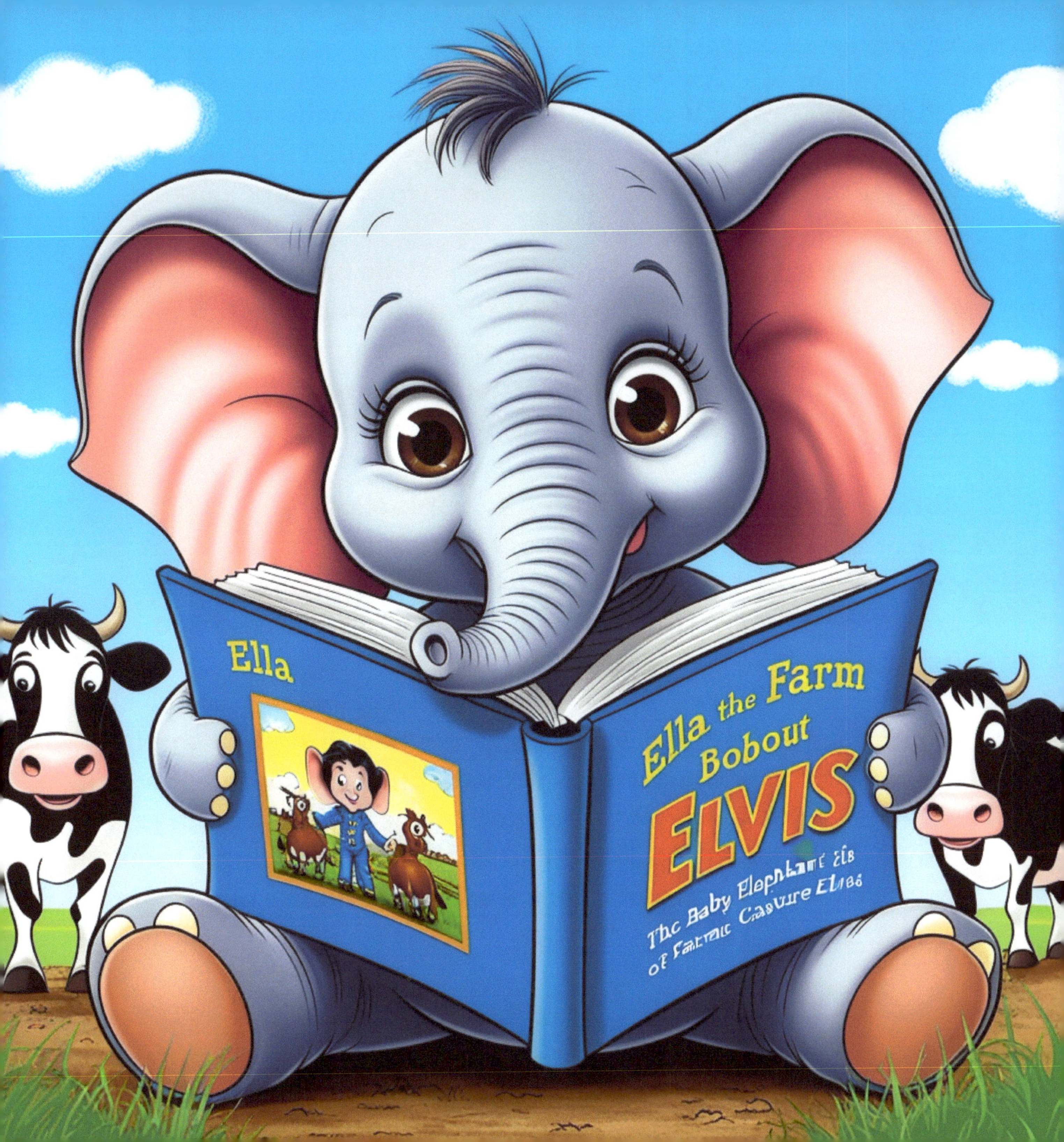
Ella
Ella the Farm
Bobout
ELVIS
The Baby Elephant
of Farm Casure Eliss

With the county fair coming up, the farmer's wife recalled the talent contest. The winner would receive $5,000 dollars. That would be enough money to save the farm from foreclosure.

Ella could win this contest, the farmer's wife predicted especially if they included some of the other farm animals. The more the farmer's wife thought of this, she became more excited. Now when she played Elvis, she rewarded the animals for any outrageous dance moves. Bananas seemed to work.

Although the mini horses preferred apple slices.
The group spent weeks on rehearsal of, "All Shook up." They coordinated and some of the cowboys and staff created costumes. Ella's looked extravagant with Elvis like wig and jumpsuit.

A staff member named Joshua approached Ella with a small stuffed elephant which was white with blue, red, and yellow polka dots. Ella immediately picked up the toy and began to play with it. Ella patted Joshua on the head as if giving a thank you. Ella loved that toy and took it everywhere. She even slept with it.

Before the fair, the staff held a luncheon with Elvis' favorite sandwich. Peanut butter and banana with Bacon and honey, grilled until golden brown and oozing butter. Miss Mary Jenkins toasted the bread before grilling but the secret is the large amount of butter and turning the bread until the bread was soaked in butter.

Finally, the day of talent contest at the fair came. Time flew and the animals were all backstage. Suddenly "All Shook Up," came on the loudspeaker and the madness began!

All the animals ran out on stage following Ella.
The crowd went nuts. Everyone stood on their chairs and started clapping. Women started screaming as Ella shook her hips. Then "Love Me Tender" started to play, and all the animal started bringing farmer's wife flowers that the farmer had brought in a basket. Over the loud speaker, "The animals at Rushing River Rescue Farm would all like to thank their mom for all her love. Even though times are rough. We know the sacrifices she has made to save our lives, especially Ella. Ella grabbed a flower and walked across the field. She approached Katy and dropped down on one knee lifting the rose up. The farmer's wife began to cry, she was so moved.

Although Elvis wore a carpet black wig with sideburns. He was an infamous brunette and was known for buying Graceland.

Just then, the speaker approached with a giant check, "Congratulations, 'Rushing River Rescue Farm' just won the grand prize of $5,000 and a donor has matched the prize of $5,000 plus more. Apparently, you're a big Elvis fan!" the speaker said to Ella.

000
Date 10-24-2024
Pay To The Order Of   Rushing River Rescue Farm $ 5,000.00
Five Thousand Dollars   Dollars
|: 000000000 |: 0000000000000||· 0000

Katy knew that Ella had just saved the farm or perhaps, she thought, it was the love for the farm that saved them all.

The farmer put his arm around his wife and leaned over into the microphone, "Thank you. Thank you very much," he said with an Elvis twang in his voice. The crowd roared approval for "Ella Loves Elvis."

Everyone seemed very happy because the rescue farm was saved. Children cheered and adults clapped in approval. Even the animals seemed happy swaying to the beat of Elvis.

Music had saved the day and the farm!

10-24-2024
000
Date
Pay To The Order Of
Rushing River Rescue Farm
$ 5,000.00
Five Thousand Dollars
Dollars
|: 00000000 |: 0000000000000||· 0000

Elvis Presley: The King of Rock 'n' Roll

Elvis Presley was born on January 8, 1935, in Tupelo, Mississippi. As a young boy, he loved listening to different kinds of music, including gospel, blues, and country. In 1954, Elvis recorded his first song, "That's All Right," which became a local hit.

Elvis quickly became famous for his energetic performances and unique style, earning him the title "King of Rock 'n' Roll." Some of his most famous songs include "Heartbreak Hotel," "Jailhouse Rock," and "Can't Help Falling in Love." He also starred in over 30 movies, like "Love Me Tender" and "Jailhouse Rock."

In 1958, Elvis joined the U.S. Army and served for two years before returning to music and acting. He continued to make hit records and movies until his death on August 16, 1977, at the age of 42.

Elvis's home, Graceland in Memphis, Tennessee, is now a popular tourist attraction. He is remembered as one of the most influential music stars of the 20th century.

www.ingramcontent.com/pod-product-compliance
Lightning Source LLC
LaVergne TN
LVHW071659180726
843512LV00002B/488

9 787091 741944